W9-CEB-227

Events That Shaped America

The
Trail of Tears

Sabrina Crewe and D. L. Birchfield

Gareth Stevens Publishing

A WORLD ALMANAC EDUCATION GROUP COMPANY

Boca Raton Public Library, Boca Raton, FL

Please visit our web site at: www.garethstevens.com
For a free color catalog describing Gareth Stevens Publishing's list of high-quality
books and multimedia programs, call 1-800-542-2595 (USA) or 1-800-387-3178
(Canada). Gareth Stevens Publishing's fax: (414) 332-3567.

Library of Congress Cataloging-in-Publication Data available upon request from publisher.
Fax (414) 336-0157 for the attention of the Publishing Records Department.

ISBN 0-8368-3400-3

This North American edition first published in 2004 by
Gareth Stevens Publishing
A World Almanac Education Group Company
330 West Olive Street, Suite 100
Milwaukee, WI 53212 USA

This edition © 2004 by Gareth Stevens Publishing.

Produced by Discovery Books
Editor: Sabrina Crewe
Designer and page production: Sabine Beaupré
Photo researcher: Sabrina Crewe
Maps and diagrams: Stefan Chabluk
Gareth Stevens editorial direction: Jim Mezzanotte
Gareth Stevens art direction: Tammy Gruenewald

Photo credits: Troy Anderson/Native Stock: cover, p. 19; Corbis: pp. 4, 6, 20 (both), 24,
25, 27 (bottom); Gilcrease Museum, Tulsa, OK: p. 17; The Granger Collection: pp. 14,
23; Native Stock: pp. 5, 22, 26, 27 (top); North Wind Picture Archives: pp. 7, 8, 9, 10,
11, 13, 15, 16, 21.

All rights reserved. No part of this book may be reproduced, stored in a retrieval system,
or transmitted in any form or by any means, electronic, mechanical, photocopying,
recording, or otherwise, without the prior written permission of the copyright holder.

Printed in the United States of America

1 2 3 4 5 6 7 8 9 08 07 06 05 04

Contents

Introduction

These Cherokee dancers are wearing a mixture of western and traditional clothing. White people in the 1800s termed Cherokees "civilized," partly because the tribe agreed to adopt some white ways of living.

An Expanding Nation

In 1830, the United States of America was quite a new country, and it wasn't as large as it is now. There were only twenty-four states, all in the East and South, and much of North America was still inhabited by the Native people who had lived there for thousands of years. In the West and Southwest, Mexico controlled huge areas.

In the early 1800s, however, the white population of the United States was growing quickly, and American settlements were moving steadily south and west. Having taken over the Native American homelands of the Northeast, white Americans were now hungry for more Indian land.

The Five Civilized Tribes

The five biggest tribes in North America's southeastern region were known as the Five **Civilized** Tribes. They were the Cherokees, Choctaws, Chickasaws, Seminoles, and Muscogees (also called the Creeks). Although the tribes had strong societies and good governments—one reason why whites called them "civilized"—Americans believed that Native cultures were inferior to their own. They wanted Indians either to move out of the way or adopt white culture.

Indian Removal

So, in 1830, the U.S. government decided to move the tribes of the Southeast farther west. Under the Indian Removal Act, the five tribes were forced to sign **treaties** with the United States. The treaties said the tribes could recreate their own **nations** on the new land. (Later, the United States wanted that land, too, and took it away.)

Throughout the 1830s, thousands of people were forced from their ancestral homelands in the Southeast and moved hundreds of miles to a place on the edge of the Great Plains. About sixty thousand people left their homes to make this journey. The death rate along the way was so high that the removals have come to be known as the "Trail of Tears."

A flame burns night and day in memory of the people who died on the Trail of Tears. This memorial stands in Red Clay, Tennessee.

Cruelest Work
"I fought through the Civil War and have seen men shot to pieces and slaughtered by thousands, but the Cherokee removal was the cruelest work I ever knew."

A U.S. Army colonel who took part in the Cherokee removal

Chapter One

The People of the Southeast

Mound Builders

People began settling and farming in the southeastern part of North America a few thousand years ago. From 500 B.C. (about 2,500 years ago), people called Mound Builders lived in the woodlands east of the Mississippi River. They were the ancestors of the Five Civilized Tribes and of many other tribes in the eastern part of North America.

Cahokia

The largest known city of the Mound Builders was Cahokia, located in what is now Illinois. The city spread over 6 square miles (15.5 square kilometers). In the area around the city, there were many smaller towns and farming villages.

The city dwellers lived under a complex class system, with spiritual leaders at the top and a working class of laborers at the bottom. Cahokia was home to about thirty thousand people. When European explorers came through in the 1680s, however, all that remained on the site was a small village.

About one hundred mounds, such as this one, still stand where the city of Cahokia once was.

Hundreds of years ago, there was a Chickasaw village on this site at Natchez Trace, Mississippi.

The Mound Builders got their name because they built large mounds. They did this by piling up dirt, one basketful at a time. The mounds were places to bury people. Some of the later ones were built in the shape of birds or snakes. Even later, people built very high mounds with wooden **temples** on top of them.

The Tribes Emerge

After about A.D. 1300 (about seven hundred years ago), the mound-building cultures slowly died out—nobody knows exactly why. But the decline of these large, centralized populations meant that many smaller tribes appeared throughout the eastern woodlands. By 1700, these included four of the Five Civilized Tribes (the Seminoles weren't a tribe yet) and several other, smaller groups.

Logic and Precision
"It seems to me they are true to their plighted faith. But we must be the same in our transactions with them. They are men who reflect, and who have more logic and precision than is commonly thought."

Governor Kerleric of Louisiana, upon meeting with Choctaws, 1753

This map was drawn in the 1770s and shows where the Five Civilized Tribes lived before they were removed. The names of the tribes were spelled a little differently than they are today, but you should be able to spot them.

Government

The Five Civilized Tribes divided the responsibility of government among their villages. Red towns were those villages that were appointed to take leadership during a war. White towns were in charge in times of peace.

Where the Tribes Lived

For hundreds of years, the Five Tribes lived in what is now the southeastern United States. The Choctaws were in Mississippi and a large part of western Alabama. The Chickasaws controlled northern Mississippi, northwestern Alabama, western Tennessee, and western Kentucky. The Cherokees inhabited the southern Appalachian Mountain region of eastern Kentucky, eastern Tennessee, northeastern Alabama, northern Georgia, and western North Carolina. The Muscogees controlled western South Carolina, most of Georgia, and much of eastern Alabama. The Seminoles broke away from the Muscogees during the 1700s and formed a separate tribe in Florida.

The tribes organized their societies as republics, allowing people to have a say in how their nations were governed. They held public meetings at which anyone had a right to speak.

Speaking Out

In Choctaw society, people wanting to speak stood beneath an **arbor** with a hole in its roof. Below that hole, through which the full heat of the Mississippi sun beat down, they were allowed to talk for as long as they stood in the heat of the sun. The others would sit in the shade and listen for as long as the speaker could keep going. They believed this method taught people to organize their thoughts, say only what needed to be said, and then sit down and be quiet.

The Role of Women

The Five Civilized Tribes were matrilineal, meaning that a person belonged to his or her mother's family. (In most white societies, a person traditionally takes his or her father's name and so could be thought of as belonging to the father's family.) Upon marriage, the husband went to live with the wife's family. Women also owned the homes and the agricultural fields, and children of a marriage were automatically members of the wife's **clan**.

The Indians of the Southeast were good farmers. This print shows a village in North Carolina in the 1500s, before white people settled in the region.

9

Chapter Two

The Coming of the Europeans

Colonists Move into Florida

In 1539, Spanish explorers and colonists began coming to the Southeast and killing the Native people who lived there. The Spanish established a colony at St. Augustine in Florida in 1565. Within 150 years, nearly all of Florida's original Native people had been wiped out.

During the 1700s, bands of Muscogees moved south into the areas of Florida that had been emptied of their Native populations. There, they gradually formed a separate group, known as the Seminoles. This nation was the fifth of the Five Civilized Tribes.

The Spanish were the first white settlers in the Southeast. They founded St. Augustine (above) in Florida in 1565.

The English and the French

When the English founded the colonies of North and South Carolina in the 1600s, they began making raids deep in what are now Georgia and Florida to capture Indians for slaves. It was a time of terror for the five tribes. During the 1700s, the British pushed westward, taking the eastern portions of Cherokee and Muscogee lands to make part of the colony of Georgia.

In 1702, the French built the town of Mobile on the edge of both Choctaw country and Muscogee country. They founded New Orleans on the southwestern edge of the Choctaw country in 1718.

White settlers took more and more tribal lands in the Southeast. This picture shows a conflict between white settlers and Indians on the eastern border of Georgia.

Colonial Power Changes Hands

In 1763, the French were expelled from the Southeast, leaving the British and Spanish in control of Native lands there. The American Revolution then ended British control in the area but created a new danger to the Native peoples: an independent American nation that wanted more land.

European Trade Goods

The Europeans brought items that Indians had never had before: steel axes and knives, pots and pans, firearms, beads, and many other things. The Indians wanted these things, and so they increased their harvest of deer hides and animal furs because the Europeans wanted those items as much as the Indians desired tools and weapons. A trading system developed that brought great changes to the traditional cultures of the tribes. The five large tribes of the Southeast adapted to these changes very well, which is another reason why Europeans called them the Five Civilized Tribes.

Chapter Three

Americans Demand Removal

Termination of Their History

"... they will in time either incorporate with us as citizens of the U.S. or remove beyond the Mississippi. The former is certainly the termination of their history most happy for themselves. ..."

Letter from President Thomas Jefferson to Governor William Henry Harrison, February 27, 1803

The Louisiana Purchase of 1803 added more than 900,000 square miles (2.3 million square kilometers) to U.S. territory.

The Louisiana Purchase

As far back as 1802, President Thomas Jefferson had thought about forcing Indian tribes to move west of the Mississippi River. An unexpected event in 1803 made this idea more possible. France sold to the United States the vast **territory** then known as Louisiana, the very region to which Jefferson wanted to banish the Indians. By the early 1800s, Americans

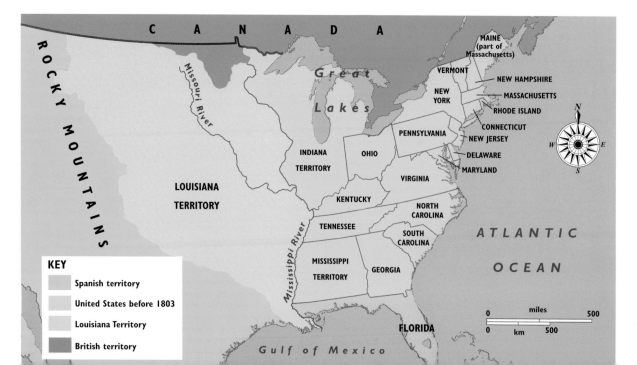

KEY
- Spanish territory
- United States before 1803
- Louisiana Territory
- British territory

were clamoring for more land in the Southeast, and the pressure on Native people was mounting.

Tecumseh's Vision

In 1811, a great Shawnee warrior named Tecumseh tried to set up a military **alliance** of all Indian tribes to stop the United States from taking their land and destroying their nations. But Chief Pushmataha of the Choctaws opposed Tecumseh and convinced the Choctaws not to join him. When Tecumseh visited the Muscogees, about half joined him, while the other half refused to do so.

Tecumseh (c. 1768–1813)

Tecumseh was born near what is now Springfield, Ohio. He was a skilled warrior widely known for his fairness and humanity. Tecumseh gained a strong following for his military alliance and, with thousands of his warriors, fought for the British against the United States in the War of 1812. On October 5, 1813, in the Battle of the Thames in Canada, Tecumseh was killed during an attack, and his dream of uniting the Indian tribes died with him.

Tecumseh (in white clothing) often helped to save the lives of white prisoners during the War of 1812.

During the War of 1812, Pushmataha, shown here, led the Choctaws in support of the United States against the British. Later, however, he opposed U.S. removal of his people.

The War of 1812

After the American Revolution was over, the British still kept soldiers in some parts of North America, and hostility continued between them and the Americans. When the War of 1812 broke out between Britain and the United States, the Indians of the Southeast took sides. Tecumseh joined the British army and led Indian warriors from different tribes in the war. Pushmataha joined the Americans, leading hundreds of Choctaw warriors in battles against Tecumseh's followers. The war ended in victory for the United States in 1815.

We Wish to Remain

"We wish to remain here, where we have grown up as the herbs of the woods, and do not wish to be transplanted into another soil."

Choctaw Chief Pushmataha, refusing to enter into a removal treaty with General Andrew Jackson, 1819

Americans Push for Removal

After the War of 1812, Americans flooded to the **frontier** to become settlers. Demands for Indian removal increased along with the white population. Georgians, meanwhile, insisted the U.S. government keep a promise it had made to them back in 1803. The government had said it would take away the remaining Indian land in Georgia so white people could have it. People in Georgia resented Indians greatly, partly because their African-American slaves kept running away to Florida and joining the Seminoles, who protected them.

Whites from Georgia [at]tacked [Se]minole [villa]ges in [Florid]a such as

[a]ngry when they found that runaway slaves had joined the Seminoles.

1828

In 1828, two important things happened. First, Georgians discovered gold in the far south of Cherokee country. They wanted the gold for themselves, so now they had another reason to demand removal of Indians from the land.

Also in 1828, Andrew Jackson was elected president of the United States. An American military leader in the War of 1812, he was a hero to the people of the frontier and had killed many Indians. Jackson had long supported Indian removal. For the Five Civilized Tribes, their worst nightmare was about to come true.

They Must Yield

"That those tribes can not exist surrounded by our settlements and in continual contact with our citizens is certain. . . . Established in the midst of another and a superior race . . . they must necessarily yield . . . and ere long disappear."

President Andrew Jackson, 1833

Chapter Four

On the Trail of Tears

The Indian Removal Act

On May 28, 1830, **Congress** passed the Indian Removal Act. The act stated that the Five Civilized Tribes were to be removed to the region that is now Oklahoma. In 1830, there was no such thing as Oklahoma, and the region was part of Arkansas Territory. Most people called it "the West."

A Kind Offer

"Rightly considered, the **policy** of the General Government toward the red man is not only liberal, but generous. . . . The General Government kindly offers him a new home. . . ."

President Andrew Jackson,
Second Annual Message to Congress, 1830

This picture shows Andrew Jackson (right) during his campaign for the presidency in 1828. As president, he persuaded Congress to pass the Indian Removal Act.

The U.S. government made a removal treaty with each of the Five Civilized Tribes. When an honest treaty is made, the two sides discuss and agree to the terms, and then both sides have to honor that agreement. With the Indian removal treaties, however, the U.S. government used threats to force the tribes to sign. It also lied to the Indians at the time and broke important promises in years to come. Under the terms of the treaties, the tribes owned the land to which they were being sent. That made no difference in later years, when Americans decided to take away the land that legally belonged to the Indian nations.

The First Removal

The first removal began in the winter of 1831 to 1832, with about four thousand Choctaws. Winter was thought to be the safest season because sickness tended to spread more in warm seasons, but it proved to be a deadly time for moving the very old and the very young. People had to travel several hundred miles in extreme cold. Many had to walk barefoot. They did not have enough food or clothes, and each person had only one thin blanket. Many froze to death in the severe weather, while others became fatally ill, lingering to die a slow death.

Choctaws and other Indians of the Southeast smoked pipes to confirm agreements. When the Choctaws signed a removal treaty in 1830, they used this pipe bowl, handed down for hundreds of years in the Choctaw nation.

Dishonest Contractors

The government hired **contractors** to organize the journey, but they did a bad job, and many Choctaws got lost. Some people had to walk through swamps that were waist deep. When the travelers ran out of food as they reached Arkansas Territory, the people who lived there raised the price of corn. Many of the surviving Choctaws who finally reached the land in the West were so weak and sick that they soon perished.

The United States decided to put the U.S. Army in charge of the next removals, but the army still had to rely on private contractors for food, clothing, and transportation. Dishonest contractors caused many deaths by buying cheap, thin blankets; by delivering cheap, spoiled food to the supply points far ahead of time, so the army wouldn't know how long it had been spoiled; and through other frauds that allowed them to pocket the money intended for removal costs. Throughout the removals, food was delivered to the wrong places, and large groups were led on routes where there was no food or shelter.

This map shows the routes taken by the Five Civilized Tribes along the Trail of Tears to the West.

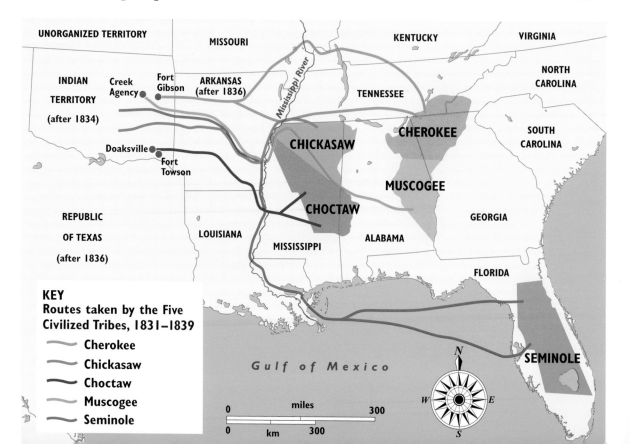

KEY
Routes taken by the Five Civilized Tribes, 1831–1839
- Cherokee
- Chickasaw
- Choctaw
- Muscogee
- Seminole

Second and Third Choctaw Removals

With the Indians in a weakened condition, sickness and disease proved deadly. During the second winter removal of about 6,000 Choctaws, the travelers were struck by **cholera**. The death toll was even higher than that of the first removal.

Only about 1,000 Choctaws could be forced into moving during the third winter, which left about 6,000 landless Choctaws in Mississippi. Most of those people eventually made their way west on their own over the next few decades. Altogether, about 2,500 of a total 11,000 removed Choctaws died either during the removals or shortly afterward.

A painting by Troy Anderson shows people along the Trail of Tears in winter. Many lost their lives in the freezing weather.

Over Frozen Ground

"The sick and feeble were carried in wagons . . . a great many ride on horseback and multitudes go on foot—even aged females, apparently nearly ready to drop into the grave, were traveling with heavy burdens attached to the back—on the sometimes frozen ground, and sometimes muddy streets, with no covering for the foot except what nature had given them."

An American traveler who saw people on the Trail of Tears near the Mississippi River, 1839

The figure of the warrior on the Great **Seal** of the Chickasaw nation (right) symbolizes the courage of the Chickasaws. The plow and sheaf of wheat on the seal of the Muscogees (below) are symbols of their great farming skills. Both seals are still used today.

Chickasaw Removal

Even after he knew the full horror of Choctaw removal, President Jackson forged ahead with the process, determined to see it through with the other tribes. When they learned what had happened to the Choctaws, the Chickasaws insisted on providing many of their own wagons and a lot of their own supplies. Most of them—about 4,000 people—were removed in 1837. Heavy rains turned the journey into a nightmare of mud and sickness, and about 600 Chickasaws died of smallpox while being moved through Arkansas.

Muscogee Removal

Before the Muscogee removals could get underway, white people swarmed into the Muscogee homeland and kicked many Muscogees out of their homes. When some Muscogees met the intruders with violence, the U.S. Army sent thousands of troops to move the Muscogees by force. In 1836, nearly 15,000 Muscogees were rounded up. About 2,500 of them, classified as **hostiles**, were put in chains and marched to the West during the winter of 1836 to 1837. The journey killed hundreds of the Muscogees. The remaining people were removed under such horrible conditions that 3,500 of them died within a year.

Osceola was a great Seminole leader who resisted the removal of his people. After many years, and a high cost in lives and money, the Americans gave up and left the remaining Seminoles in Florida.

Seminole Removal

In 1832, one faction of the Seminoles negotiated a removal treaty, the Treaty of Payne's Landing, and some Seminoles left Florida. Many Seminoles refused to be removed, however, and fought the Americans in Florida for years.

Burying a Child in Stranger-Land

"She could only carry her dying child in her arms a few miles farther, and then, she must stop in a stranger-land and consign her much loved babe to the cold ground, and that without pomp or ceremony, and pass on with the multitude. . . . When I past the last detachment of those suffering exiles and thought that my native countrymen had thus expelled them from their native soil and their much loved homes . . . I turned from the sight with feelings which language cannot express and wept like childhood then."

An American traveler watching people on the Trail of Tears, 1839

John Ross was the leader of the many Cherokees who resisted removal. Ross was finally forced to move, however, along with thousands of other Cherokees.

Cherokee Removal

A small minority of the Cherokees signed a removal treaty in 1835 and moved to the West. The large majority of Cherokees, however, under Chief John Ross, refused to acknowledge the treaty and stayed.

In 1838, therefore, the U.S. Army swept into the Cherokee nation with 7,000 troops and rounded up most of the Cherokees. Thousands of people were held in prison camps under terrible conditions until the Cherokee removal could start.

By this time, the tragedy of the removals had attracted the attention of the American people. Many white Americans

Dragged from Their Homes

"Men working in the fields were arrested and driven to the **stockades**. Women were dragged from their homes by soldiers whose language they could not understand. Children were often separated from their parents and driven into the stockades with the sky for a blanket and the earth for a pillow. And often the old and the infirm were prodded with bayonets to hasten them to the stockade."

Private John G. Burnett, a U.S. Army soldier who participated in the Cherokee removal

No Hope

"We are in trouble, Sir, our hearts are very heavy. . . .
We have no hope unless you will help us . . . we ask that you
not send us . . . at this time of year. If you do we shall die,
our wives will die or our children will die. . . ."

*Petition of one hundred prominent Cherokees
to General Winfield Scott, 1838*

protested against the policy, but the government ignored them. Most of the Cherokees were removed at one time, during the winter of 1838 to 1839, in 13 groups of about 1,000 each. The total death toll, in the camps and on the removal journey, was about 4,000 people.

By the end of the 1830s, about 60,000 southeastern Indians had been removed to the West. In all, the Trail of Tears took the lives of about 15,000 people.

The removal of the Cherokees, shown here, killed nearly one-third of the 13,000 people sent along the Trail of Tears in the winter of 1838 to 1839.

Chapter Five

After Removal

The five tribes formed their own nations and governments in Indian Territory. This 1880 meeting of twenty-four tribes was held at the Muscogee council house.

Life and Death in a New Land

In the first few years, life in the new land proved almost as deadly as the removals had been. The United States had promised food and farming supplies for a year, but many people found themselves simply dumped in an uninhabited region without food, clothing, or shelter.

New Constitutions

Despite losing thousands of their people to starvation and illness during the first few years, the tribes survived and made the best of what little they had. They wrote new **constitutions** for their governments and organized school systems for their children. People cleared farmland, planted crops, and began bringing order and stability back into their lives. In Indian Territory, as it was now called, the tribes were allowed to govern themselves without American interference.

The Civil War

All of that changed with the outbreak of the American Civil War in 1861. Both northern and southern armies swept through Indian Territory, causing terrible damage and death. When the war ended, floods of white settlers entered the Indian nations. By the 1870s, the Indians were outnumbered by Americans in their own countries.

Broken Treaties and a New State

The whites began clamoring to abolish the Indian nations and form a state in Indian Territory. In 1907, the state of Oklahoma was created, and members of the Five Civilized Tribes were forced to become citizens of the new state. The promise that they would always have their nations in the West was broken, like all the other promises that had been made to the tribes by the U.S. government. The peoples of the Indian Territory watched helplessly as their nations were destroyed and their land was taken away.

A Promise Broken

". . . no territory or state shall ever have a right to pass laws for the government of the Choctaw Nation of Red People and their descendants; and no part of the land granted them shall ever be embraced in any territory or state. . . ."

Government of the United States, Article IV, Choctaw Removal Treaty of 1830

In 1893, the U.S. government offered millions of acres of Indian Territory to white settlers. This photograph was taken as the settlers rushed in to claim Cherokee land.

Conclusion

This is the government seat of the removed Chickasaw people, who are trying to maintain the traditions and rights of their nation.

The Tragedy of Removal

The Trail of Tears, and what happened after it, was one of the most tragic and destructive episodes in the history of the Cherokees, Choctaws, Chickasaws, Muscogees, and Seminoles. The decision for removal was also one of the cruelest choices made in the history of the United States.

A Heavy Weight

"The history of the Cherokee removal of 1838 . . . may well exceed in weight of grief and pathos any other passage in American history."

James Mooney, Historical Sketch of the Cherokee, *1900*

The Oklahoma Tribes Reform Their Governments

In the 1970s, the tribes in Oklahoma were finally allowed to reform their governments. The Five Civilized Tribes wrote new constitutions and elected tribal leaders for the first time since Oklahoma became a state. The tribal governments are now trying to regain many of the ordinary powers of government that were lost.

Those Who Stayed Behind

Early in the twentieth century, the U.S. government became aware that some southeastern Indians remained in the Southeast. Descendants of people who had avoided removal, they were living in swamps and other remote and unwanted areas.

The government started buying parcels of land so those Indians might have some tribal lands again, however small. By mid-century, Choctaws living in Mississippi were able to organize their own government, write a constitution, and gain recognition as the Mississippi Band of Choctaw Indians. Other eastern bands of the Five Civilized Tribes reappeared, including the eastern Cherokees in North Carolina, the Seminoles in southern Florida, and the Poarch Creeks (a Muscogee band) and Mowa Choctaws in Alabama.

The Seminole child (above) keeps her culture alive with traditional clothes. The Cherokee elders (below) continue to make baskets as their ancestors did.

Damage Done

In spite of these steps forward, the damage to some of North America's most important cultures remains. The Trail of Tears resulted in the Five Civilized Tribes losing about one-fourth of their people. Many of the people who died were old people—the elders—who possessed the cultural knowledge of their tribes. When they died on the Trail of Tears, much of their knowledge died with them.

500 B.C.	Mound-building civilizations arise in Mississippi River valley.
A.D. 1300	Mound-building civilizations reach their height.
1565	First permanent Spanish colony established at St. Augustine in Florida.
1700s	Some Muscogees move to Florida and form Seminole tribe.
1802	President Thomas Jefferson makes first mention of Indian Removal.
1803	April 23: U.S. government promises Georgia it will take away Indian land in the state.
	Louisiana Purchase.
1811	Tecumseh attempts to form Indian military alliance among southern tribes.
1812–1815	War of 1812.
1813	Tecumseh is killed at the Battle of the Thames.
1828	Georgians discover gold in Cherokee country and gold rush begins.
	Andrew Jackson is elected President of United States.
1830	May 28: Congress passes Indian Removal Act.
1831–1832	First Choctaw removal begins Trail of Tears.
1832–1833	Second Choctaw removal.
1833–1834	Third Choctaw removal.
1834	Indian Territory is officially organized.
	Partial Seminole removal.
1836–1837	Muscogee removal.
1837	Chickasaw removal.
1838–1839	Cherokee removal.
1861–1865	American Civil War.
1907	Oklahoma becomes a state and Indian nations in Indian Territory are abolished.

Things to Think About and Do

Foreign Invasion

North America was the home of millions of North Americans for several thousand years before Europeans arrived and took over the continent by force. Imagine that, today, a group of people, speaking a different language and armed with superior weapons, comes to take over your country and begins killing your family and friends. Describe your thoughts and feelings and how you would react.

Treaty

Indians and white Americans in the 1800s had very different ideas about land ownership. Find out what you can about their views. Then write a treaty that you think is fair. It should reflect the situation at the time, which was that thousands of whites, expecting to obtain land for settlement and farming, were arriving in a country that was already the homeland of many tribes.

On the Trail of Tears

Imagine that you and your family are from one of the Five Civilized Tribes and have been forced to move west on the Trail of Tears. Write an account of your journey and arrival in a new land.

Glossary

alliance: nations or groups joined together for a common purpose.

arbor: shelter made of branches and leaves.

cholera: highly infectious disease that affects the intestine and can kill large numbers of people when an epidemic breaks out.

civilized: having a high level of culture and development.

clan: division of a tribe consisting of a small group that has a duty to provide services—such as burials—for its members, as well as many other social functions.

Congress: official body of the United States government that makes laws.

constitution: basic rules of government for a nation.

contractor: person given a contract, or agreement, to perform a service for a fee.

frontier: edge of something known or settled. The U.S. frontier moved west across North America as white settlement expanded.

hostile: unfriendly. The U.S. government termed as "hostiles" all Indians who resisted white control or settlement in any way.

nation: people of a particular country, which in Indian terms means a large tribe; also the geographical territory of a tribe or group.

policy: plan or way of doing things that is decided upon in advance and then used in managing situations or making decisions.

seal: stamp bearing an official symbol of a government or nation.

stockade: enclosed area, usually surrounded by thick wooden posts, for holding prisoners.

temple: building used for spiritual purposes.

territory: land claimed by a particular group. Regions such as Arkansas Territory and Indiana Territory in the 1800s were claimed and governed by the United States but were not part of any states.

treaty: agreement between two groups or nations after negotiation, often at the end of a period of conflict.

Further Information

Books

Birchfield, D. L. *Seminole* (Native American Peoples). Gareth Stevens, 2003.

Bruchac, Joseph. *Trail of Tears* (Step Into Reading). Random House, 1999.

Burke, Rick. *Andrew Jackson* (American Lives: Presidents). Heinemann Library, 2003.

Kamma, Anne. *If You Lived with the Cherokee* (If You). Scholastic, 1998.

Koestler-Grack, Rachel A. *Tecumseh: 1768–1813* (American Indian Biographies). Bridgestone, 2003.

Web Sites

www.choctawnation.com Official web site of the Choctaw nation offers historical information about the tribe.

www.nps.gov/trte National Park Service web site for the Trail of Tears National Historic Trail, which has preserved parts of the Cherokee Trail of Tears and sites along the way.

www.rosecity.net/tears/ Tourist web site offers information about the Trail of Tears and many relevant links.

Useful Addresses

National Trail of Tears Association
1110 North University, Suite 143
Little Rock, AR 72207
Telephone: (501) 666-9032

Index

BOCA RATON PUBLIC LIBRARY, FLORIDA

3 3656 0440693 0

J 975.00497557 Cre
Crewe, Sabrina.
The Trail of Tears /